THE SECOND BOOK OF MEZZO-SOPRANO/ALTO SOLOS

compiled by Joan Frey Boytim

G. SCHIRMER, Inc.

DISTRIBUTED BY

HAL•LEONARD®
CORPORATION
7777 W. BLUEMOUND RD. P.O. BOX 13819 MILWAUKEE, WI 53213

PREFACE

The eight volumes that comprise "The First Book of Solos" and "The First Book of Solos—Part II" were compiled to provide a great variety of song literature at the same basic level of difficulty for students at the beginning stages of voice study. The four volumes in "The Second Book of Solos" are designed to contribute to musical and vocal development at the next progressive level of study.

The majority of these songs require more vocal sophistication than those found in the earlier volumes. Singers using this set will be exposed to songs with wider ranges that require more vocal flexibility and vocal control, and that make greater use of the dramatic qualities of the voice. The student who can sing many of the songs in the "The First Book" and "The First Book—Part II" will be ready for the challenges found in "The Second Book of Solos."

The general format of songs remains the same as the previous collections, with a representative group of songs in English, Italian, German, and French from various periods of music history, as well as selected sacred solos. Added are several songs from Gilbert and Sullivan operettas and solos from the oratorio repertoire. Numerous pieces previously available only in single sheet form and many songs that for some time have been out of print are included.

I want to thank Richard Walters for encouraging the development of this practical song literature series. The twelve books, taken together, provide a comprehensive, inexpensive collection of 400 songs for the voice teacher and student.

Joan Frey Boytim

About the Compiler...

Since 1968, Joan Frey Boytim has owned and operated a full-time voice studio in Carlisle, Pennsylvania, where she has specialized in developing a serious and comprehensive curriculum and approach to teaching and coaching adolescent and community adult students. Her teaching experience has also included music and choral instruction at the junior high and senior high levels, and voice instruction at the college level. She is the author of the widely used bibliography, *Solo Vocal Repertoire for Young Singers* (a publication of NATS), and, as a nationally recognized expert on teaching beginning vocal study, is a frequent speaker and clinician on the topic.

CONTENTS

AN DIE MUSIK

(To Music)

Franz von Schober
English version by Gustave Reese

Franz Schubert

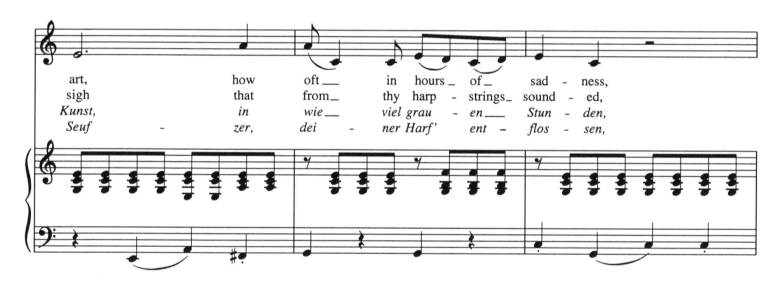

AN DIE NACHTIGALL

(To a Nightingale)

Ludwig Heinrich Christoph Hölty

Johannes Brahms

Printed in the U.S.A by G. Schirmer, Inc.

schmel- - - - -zend__ Ach.
melt- - - - -ing__ sigh.

Dann flieht der Schlaf von neu-em die-ses La - ger, ich
Then bless-ed sleep once more de-serts my cham-ber, Mine

star - re dann mit nas-sem Blick und
eyes I raise, Eyes full of tears, and

GREAT PEACE HAVE THEY WHICH LOVE THY LAW

from the Psalms

James H. Rogers

AU BORD DE L'EAU

(At the Water's Edge)

Sully Prudhomme
English words by Marion Farquhar

Gabriel Fauré

Printed in the U.S.A by G. Schirmer, Inc.

ser, A l'ho - ri - zon s'il fume un toit de chau - me,___
blow, If far off thatch on a cot-tage is fum - ing,___

Le voir___ fu - mer, Aux a - len - tours si quel-que fleur em -
To watch the fume, And,close at hand if a flow-er is

bau - me,___ S'en em - bau - mer, En - tendre au
bloom - ing,___ To breath the bloom, When through the

pied du saule où l'eau mur - mu - re,___ L'eau mur - mu - rer, Ne pas sen -
wil-low roots, wa - ter is sigh - ing,___ To hear it sigh, And not to

Sans se las - ser, Sen - tir l'a - mour, de - vant tout ce qui
Wea - ri - ness pass, And feel that love, be - fore all that is

pas - se, Ne point pas - ser,___
pass - ing, Will nev - er pass,___

Sen - tir l'a - mour, de - vant tout ce qui pas - se,___
And feel that love, be - fore all that is pass - ing,___

Ne point pas - ser! _____
Will nev - er pass! _____

LES BERCEAUX

(The Cradles)

Sully Prudhomme
English version by Marion Farquhar

Gabriel Fauré

Le long du quai ___ les grands ___ vais-seaux,
Far down the quay ___ the ves - sels lie,

Que la hou-le-in-cli - ne en si-len - - ce,___ Ne
On the tide so si - lent-ly swing - - ing;___ As

pren - nent pas gar - - de aux ___ ber-ceaux,
yet un-a-ware ___ of cra - dles there,

Printed in the U.S.A by G. Schirmer, Inc.

Que la main des fem - mes ba - lan - ce.
Rock-ing to the rhy - thm of sing - ing.

cre - scen - do poco a

Mais vien - dra le jour des a - dieux,
But there comes le the day of good-bye,

cre - scen - do poco a

poco

Car il faut que les fem - mes pleu - rent,
For, they say, wo - men must be cry - ing,

poco

cresc. molto

Et que les hom - mes cu - ri - eux
And men must go, rest - less to know,

cresc. molto

UN CERTO NON SO CHE

(There's one, I know him not)

English version by Theodore Baker

Antonio Vivaldi

DU BIST DIE RUH'

(Thou Art Repose)

Friedrich Rückert

English translation by Theodore Baker

Franz Schubert

SUPPORT

hier _____ mein Aug' und_ Herz, _____ mein Aug' und_ Herz.

here: _____ Mine eye and_ heart, _____ mine eye and_ heart.

Kehr' ein bei mir, und schlie - sse du still hin - ter

En - ter thou in, And soft - ly close On all my

dir die Pfor - ten zu. Treib' an - dern Schmerz _____

woes The door with - in. Let pain de - part, _____

EYE HATH NOT SEEN

from The Holy City

Alfred Robert Gaul

the things which God hath pre-pared, pre - pared for them that_ love

espressivo *espr.*

mf

Più mosso ♩=88

Him.

mf *cresc.*

mf *f*

For He hath pre - pared ___ for them ___ a cit - y, whose

f

build - er and mak - er is God, He hath pre - pared, ___ pre-

HEARD YE HIS VOICE?

(from the Russian of Puschkin)
Translated by Arthur Westbrook

Anton Rubinstein

IM HERBST

(In Autumn)

Wolfgang Müller
Translation by Theodore Baker

Robert Franz

HUSHED THE SONG OF THE NIGHTINGALE

(Il s'est tu, le charmant rossignol)

J. Nikitine
French by Calvocoressi
English by Constance Purdy

Alexander Gretchaninoff

I, _____ this night fill'd with gold - en dreams _____
Cet - te nuit, et ce rê - ve si beau _____

_____ Would pro - long with - out end, with - out end. _____
que ne puis je les vivre à ja - mais. _____

I SOUGHT THE LORD

Psalm xxxiv: 4
Psalm cxxi: 8
Revelations xxi: 4

Frederick Stevenson

Printed in the U.S.A by G. Schirmer, Inc.

THE JOLLY JOLLY BREEZE

John Eccles

The jol - ly jol - ly breeze That comes whis - tling thro' the trees From

all _____ the bliss - ful _ re - gion brings Per - fumes _____ up -

-on _ its spi - cy _ wings. The -on _ its spi - cy _ wings. With its wan -

KIND FORTUNE SMILES

Ariel's song in The Tempest
by William Shakespeare

Henry Purcell

Kind ———— For - tune

smiles, and she has yet ————————— in — store for thee some

LILACS

English version by Henry G. Chapman

Sergei Rachmaninoff

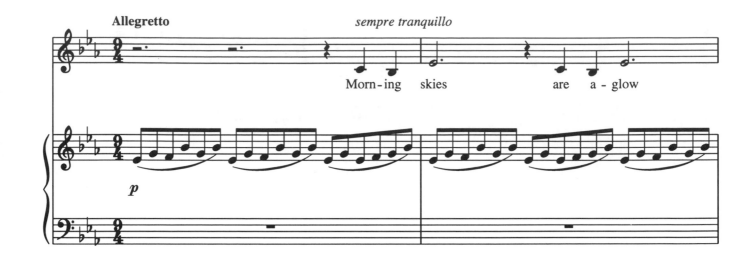

Morn-ing skies are a-glow

While the li - lac - trees blow, And I breathe of the fresh morn-ing

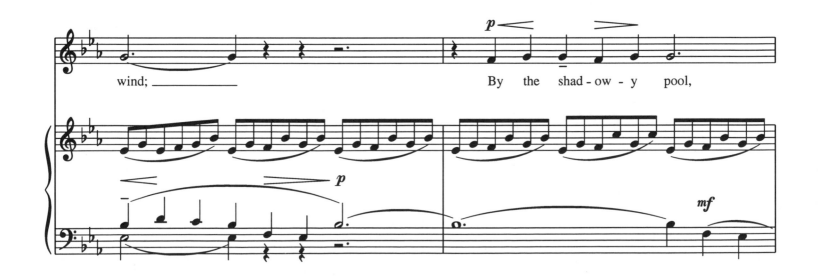

wind; _____ By the shad-ow - y pool,

Where it's dew - y and cool, I must see if my for - tune I'll

find.

Ah, of luck there's scant dole, _____ Yet it's ev - 'ry-one's

LITTLE BUTTERCUP

from H.M.S. Pinafore

Words by W. S. Gilbert

Arthur Sullivan

I'm called lit-tle But-ter-cup, Dear lit-tle But-ter-cup.

Though I could nev-er tell why; But still I'm call'd But-ter-cup,

Poor lit-tle But-ter-cup, Sweet lit-tle But-ter-cup I. I've

pret - ty po - lo-nies, And ex - cel-lent pep-per-mint drops._____ Then

buy of your But-ter-cup, Dear lit - tle But-ter-cup, Sail-ors should ne-ver be shy—

So buy of your But-ter-cup, Poor lit-tle But-ter-cup, Come, of your But-ter-cup

buy.____

LOVE, I HAVE WON YOU

Harold Simpson

Landon Ronald

Agitato e con molto passione.

Love,_____ I have won you and held you In a life - - long quick-en-ing

dream;_____ When the mea - dows sprang fair with

flow - ers And the riv er was all a gleam.

Warm_____ shone the sun-light a - round us, And

clear_____ were the skies a - bove, Till the

A LULLABY

Cahal O'Byrne

Hamilton Harty

rose - strewn........ strand...... bath'd in glist - 'ning dew,........

........bath'd in glist - - - - - - - 'ning

dim.

dew.

mf

I'll make you a nest, a soft, warm

nest, In my heart's core,........ *A - lan - niv as - thore,*........When

rall. un poco

"Alanniv asthore" is translated as "my sweetheart" or "my baby"

ORPHEUS WITH HIS LUTE

William Shakespeare

Arthur Sullivan

Or - pheus with his lute, with his lute made trees And the

moun - tain tops that freeze Bow them-selves when he did

PASTORALE

Regnard
Translated by J.F. Reginald

Georges Bizet

molto rall.

p

dear, Give___ me,___ I pray_____ thee, one ten -
re lais - se - moi pren - - - dre un ten -

colla voce

p

tr   3   *a tempo*

der kiss."___
dre bai - ser!"___

pp

p

p

p

p

The maid - en so
La belle,___ à l'ins -

bright _____
tant _____

An-swered Co - lin with
Ré - pond à son ber -

82

PATIENTLY HAVE I WAITED

from The Christmas Oratorio

Camille Saint-Saëns

PLEASURE'S GENTLE ZEPHYRS PLAY

George Frideric Handel

DECEIT.

Plea - sure's gen-tle ze - phyrs play,......... Spread thy sail, make no de - lay,...........

.... To the land where mirth and joy................. for-ev-er reign.

Plea - sure's gen - tle ze - phyrs play, play,...............

play, ... spread thy sail, ...

spread thy....

sail, make no de - lay, to the land where mirth and joy for ev - er reign,

mirth and joy .... for ev - er reign.

Fine.

Let.......... no fool - ish fears...... con-found thee, Taste the joys that

now sur - round thee, Nor let Plea-sure smile in vain,

Taste the joys that now......... sur - round thee, Nor let

Plea-sure smile in vain, Nor let Plea-sure

D.C.

smile in vain,............... Nor let Plea-sure smile in vain.

D.C.

TE SOUVIENS-TU?

(Remembrance)

Translated by Alexander Blaess

Benjamin Godard

Allegro (♩ = 100)

PIANO

Dost thou re-call thy wist-ful prom - ise,
Te sou - viens - tu de ta pro - mes - se?

Dost thou re-call the hap-py past?
Te sou - viens - tu des ans pas - sés?

Dost thou re-call our thrill-ing rap - - ture,
Te sou - viens - tu de no - trei - vres - se

Printed in the U.S.A by G. Schirmer, Inc.

When in my arms I held thee fast?_____ Oh, guard me well thy heart's af-
Quand nos bras é-taient en-la-cés?_____ Oh! gar-de-moi bien ta ten-

fec - tion; In bit-ter want I need thy kiss!_____
dres - se, J'ai tant be-soin de tes bai-sers!_____

Dost thou re-call my tear-ful sad - ness,
Te sou-viens-tu de ma tris-tes - se

When for one day we had to part?
Lors-que je par-tais pour un jour?

SILVER'D IS THE RAVEN HAIR

from Patience

W. S. Gilbert

Arthur Sullivan

com - ing bye   and bye!

Fa - ding is the ta - per— waist,

Shapeless grows the shape-ly— limb,   And al-though se - vere-ly— laced,

THE SMILING HOURS

from Hercules

George Frideric Handel

Da Capo al Fine.

THOU SHALT BRING THEM IN

from Israel in Egypt

George Frideric Handel

TO THE CHILDREN

English version by Rosa Newmarch

Sergei Rachmaninoff

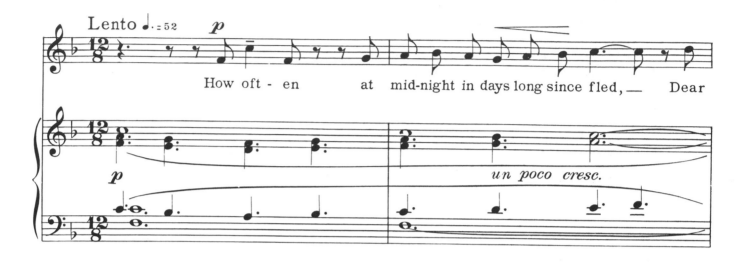

How oft - en   at mid-night in days long since fled, — Dear

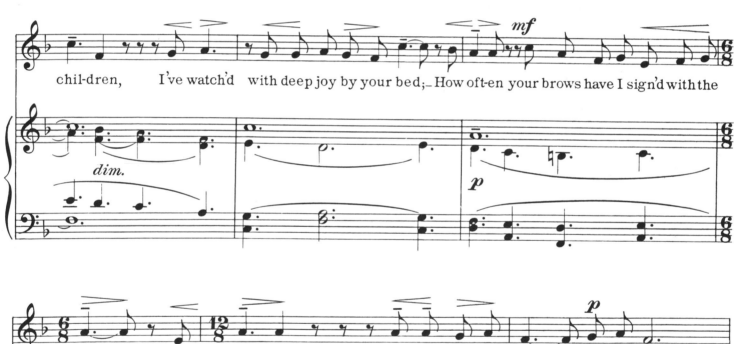

chil-dren,   I've watch'd   with deep joy by your bed;— How oft-en your brows have I sign'd with the

Cross, — And   pray'd there: God keep you from sor - row and loss;

But now, in the nurs-'ry reigns still-ness and gloom,— Gone, gone the glad

voi-ces, no sound in the room;— No lamp lights the i-con that hangs by the

door;— My heart aches— The chil-dren are chil-dren no

more!— What an-guish to lose them for-ev—er!

VAAREN

(Spring)

A. O. Vinje
English version by Willis Wager

Edvard Grieg

Printed in the U.S.A by G. Schirmer, Inc.

VERBORGENHEIT

(Secrecy)

Eduard Mörike
Translated by Charles Fonteyn Manney

Hugo Wolf

WE SING TO HIM

Henry Purcell

Broadly, not too slowly

(8va bass optional)

We sing to Him, whose wis-dom formed the ear, Our songs, let Him who gave us voic-es, hear. We joy in God, who is the spring of mirth, Who loves the har-mo-ny of Heaven and Earth. Our hum-ble son-nets shall that praise re-hearse, Who is the mu-sic of the U-ni-verse.

WHERE CORALS LIE

from Sea Pictures
Richard Garnett

Edward Elgar

lips are like a sun - set glow,.................... Thy

smile is like a morn - ing sky, ... Yet

leave me, leave me, let me go And see the land where corals lie,......... The

land, ... the land .... where cor - als lie ....

CON RAUCO MORMORIO

(With Mournful Sounds of Weeping)

George Frideric Handel

Fine

With sad and bro - ken sigh - ing The
E in tron - chi e me - sti ac - cen - ti *Fann'*

ech - oes, the ech - oes come re - ply - ing
e - co *Fann' e - co miei la - men - ti*

From cav - erns and moun - tains
E gli an - tri, *E i - mon - ti,*

126